The Woman's Guide to

Living Your Dreams

by

Shanna Beaman

Beaman Company, LLC

A Utah Company

Dedication

*I want to thank my husband
for working hard and for his support,
and my children for being so wonderful
while I wrote this guide.*

Thank you for believing in me!

Contents

Additional forms can be found and printed at www.dustingoffdreams.com
Go to the Tools tab and click on <u>Living Your Dreams</u>
Enter the password: dreamweaving

Introduction

I am writing this book, just for women, because I know that we have very little discretionary time for ourselves and for our dreams. I am going to teach you an easy and effective way to achieve your dreams with proper planning and time management.

In the Part I of this guide, I am going to go over some important basics about dreams and goals. In Part II, I will walk through how to write your dreams and set up an effective strategy for them. In Part III, you are going to learn how to manage your time and learn about *Dream Weaving*.

In Part IV, I provide a plethora of other useful tips. My inspiration for this guide was to provide a multitude of ideas that you can reference in your daily life, in an easy-to-read format. I hope that you will draw from this Part on a regular basis to help you stay motivated and find time in your life for your family *and* for your dreams.

Maintaining a strong family unit is a priority, for most, and I have found ways to keep my family strong and still find time for my dreams and goals; I want to share this information with you, with the hope that some of these ideas will work for you. Writing down your dreams and having a purpose to achieve them will benefit you, your family and everyone around you.

By using the quick and simple forms provided in this guide, you can begin the journey that will lead you to your dreams, committing as little as 10 minutes each day for *Dream Weaving*. This is an easy reference manual that will take you farther than you ever thought possible!

You deserve the best….now go get it!

❧ *Believe in yourself.*
You will succeed when you believe! ❧

Part I

All About Dreams and Goals

"And the day came when the risk to remain tight in a bud
was more painful than the risk it took to blossom."
Anais Nin

Dusting off your dreams

This is where your journey begins

Chapter One

Dreams and Goals

"Don't be afraid of the space between your dreams and reality.
If you can dream it, you can make it so."
Belva Davis

Dreams and goals go hand-in-hand; when you don't have a dream, there is no need to have a goal. When you do have a dream, then a goal will help you reach it. The goal is the vehicle that you will use to achieve your dream.

❖ A dream is a something you yearn for; a wish.

❖ A goal is a dream with a plan and a deadline.

When you combine your dream with a goal, you have a tangible result and here are some fun and quick definitions of a goal:

- A life plan
- A dream with a deadline
- A wish for which you have an aim
- Your life's purpose mapped out on paper
- An aspiration with a plan of action and the end in mind
- A deep desire with a clearly defined path
- An ambition you have committed to

A goal cannot be described as:

- An intention
- A daydream
- A fantasy
- Hoping for luck
- A wish without a plan

Dreams make life more delightful and joyous and they give you something to look forward to.

Stop right now and take 30 seconds to close your eyes and dream. Think of what you want to be, what you want to do and what you want to have.

*❧ A goal is simply the vehicle
you use to achieve your dreams ❧*

Chapter Two

Why Setting Goals is Important

You use a roadmap on a trip in your car;
why wouldn't you use a roadmap on the trip called life?
Tom Beaman

I know the term 'goal setting' seems so boring and it probably sounds a lot like work but I don't want to you think that way; think of goal setting as a fun game that you are setting up and you are going to win!

By setting a goal, you are setting up your game. You can't play the game if it's not set up and you can't win if you don't play.

"Setting up" your goals is important because if your goals are clearly defined and well written, they will enable you to achieve your dreams. We will discuss the goal setting process later.

Below are some of the many reasons why goal setting is important and why you should set them:

- Goals create enthusiasm because you are excited to pursue your success
- Goals make you happy because your mind is alive and it has something encouraging to focus on
- Goals give you confidence and, with confidence, you believe in yourself
- Goals create discipline from within because you have a plan and you know exactly what you must do each day and you just do it
- Goal setting, along with planning, helps you use your time more efficiently creating additional time for taking action on your dreams
- Goals eliminate negativity because you are motivated to succeed and you do not fear anything that stands in your way

- Goals give you a reason for action, helping you identify *why* you are working toward your dream
- Goals provide direction and a strategy so you will know which way to go and exactly what your next move is
- Goal setting creates constructive thought that forms ideas and creates action that you will experience immediately after writing your goal

You *will* live your dreams and the feeling of dream achievement is extraordinary!

Now, let's look at the consequences of *not* setting your goals:

- You will wander aimlessly, wondering which way to go
- You won't know what your next move is
- You are not excited because all you have is a far-fetched dream
- You are unsure about yourself and your abilities
- You will believe others when they say "You'll never do that"
- You will allow obstacles to take away your focus from your dreams

You are probably wondering "If setting goals works and a written goal truly helps you achieve your dreams, then why don't more people set them?" Below are the reasons why I believe most people don't set goals:

- They look at it as a task
- They think it sounds boring
- They don't know where to begin
- They don't know that a goal *is* the vehicle to your dreams
- They don't know how to set goals
- They don't realize the importance of a plan
- They don't make the time to write anything down
- They procrastinate
- They let intimidation rule their lives
- They are afraid of failure

When you are sincere about dream attainment, goals are your vehicle, your game board, to that attainment. You will be a better person, mother and wife when you start achieving the dreams that have great meaning to you and it will positively impact you and the ones you love.

With proper goal setting skills, you have the opportunity to do, be and have anything you want in life!

You are extremely more likely to achieve your dreams when you have clearly defined goals

Chapter Three

Who Has Dreams and Goals

"If I had one wish for my children, it would be that each of them would reach for goals that have meaning for them as individuals."
Lillian Gordy Carter

Everyone has dreams. Dreams keep you vibrant and alive; they give you willpower, hope and ambition.

Some people don't take action on their dreams and they just let them fade away. To me, it is disheartening when people let go of their dreams. Make a promise to yourself now that you will not be one of those people; that you will keep your dreams burning brightly!

Do it now. Close your eyes, relax and make a mental promise to yourself.

Very few individuals take the time to set proper and effective goals, but everyone should set goals because everyone has dreams, no matter how small they may be. Studies show that only 3% of adults have written goals.

These are the people who are most likely to set goals:

- You, because you have dreams and are reading this guide
- Elite and novice athletes
- Professionals
- Business Owners
- Entrepreneurs
- People in the sales profession
- Coaches and Mentors
- Individuals who have already experienced success from setting previous goals

The success rate on those who do not have a clearly defined plan to reach their dreams diminishes to almost zero percent.

I want you to plan your life today; to start setting up your game. *You* are now (or will be) one of the 3% of individuals who set goals and we'll get started on setting goals in Part II.

Until then, I have a just a few more important things to share, so keep dreaming until we get there!

*Everyone should set goals
and follow their dreams*

Chapter Four

Living a Balanced Life

"When you are balanced and when you listen and attend to the needs of your body, mind, and spirit, your natural beauty comes out."
Christy Turlington

A balanced life is when you are well rounded; when you are experiencing success uniformly in all areas of your life.

To live the most fulfilling life, you should have dreams and goals in every area, concentrating on the areas that need the most improvement. By focusing on and setting goals in the areas of life that need attention; you will bring balance into your life.

There are 5 main areas in life to have dreams *and* balance:

1. Health

    - Sleep
    - Physical activity
    - Healthy weight
    - Proper hydration
    - Balanced meals
    - Supplementation
    - Proactive wellness and checkups

2. Financial

    - Job
    - Career
    - Self employment
    - Entrepreneurship

- Multiple streams of income
- Ability to pay all your monthly bills
- Retirement
- Budgeting
- Debt free
- Financially free

3. Family and relationship

- Time with children
- Time with spouse or partner
- Time with extended family
- Time with friends
- Circle of influence
- Group activities
- Group membership
- Team involvement

4. Spiritual

- Inner Peace
- Charity
- Religion
- God
- Meditation
- Introspect

5. Self improvement

- Attitude
- Belief in yourself
- School
- Reading
- Audio
- Seminars
- Training
- Mentors

You must have balance in your life and I am going to explain why in the following examples:

1. If you are so focused on building your wealth that you neglect your family, you may suffer negative consequences with your husband or miss out on your children's growing years.

2. If you neglect your health now, you may be limiting yourself to the joy of quality family time or retirement later in life due to conditions that transpire because of this inattention to your wellbeing.

A balanced life adds to your happiness and helps ensure a positive outlook on life, and happiness and optimism will be contributing factors in the achievement your dreams.

[The fun exercise on the next page is designed to create a visual picture that will help you determine where to focus some of your efforts to bring your life into balance.]

Well Rounded

Financial
10 9 8 7 6 5 4 3 2 1

Relationships
1 2 3 4 5 6 7 8 9 10

You

Health
1 2 3 4 5 6 7 8 9 10

Self Improvement
1 2 3 4 5 6 7 8 9 10

Spiritual
1 2 3 4 5 6 7 8 9 10

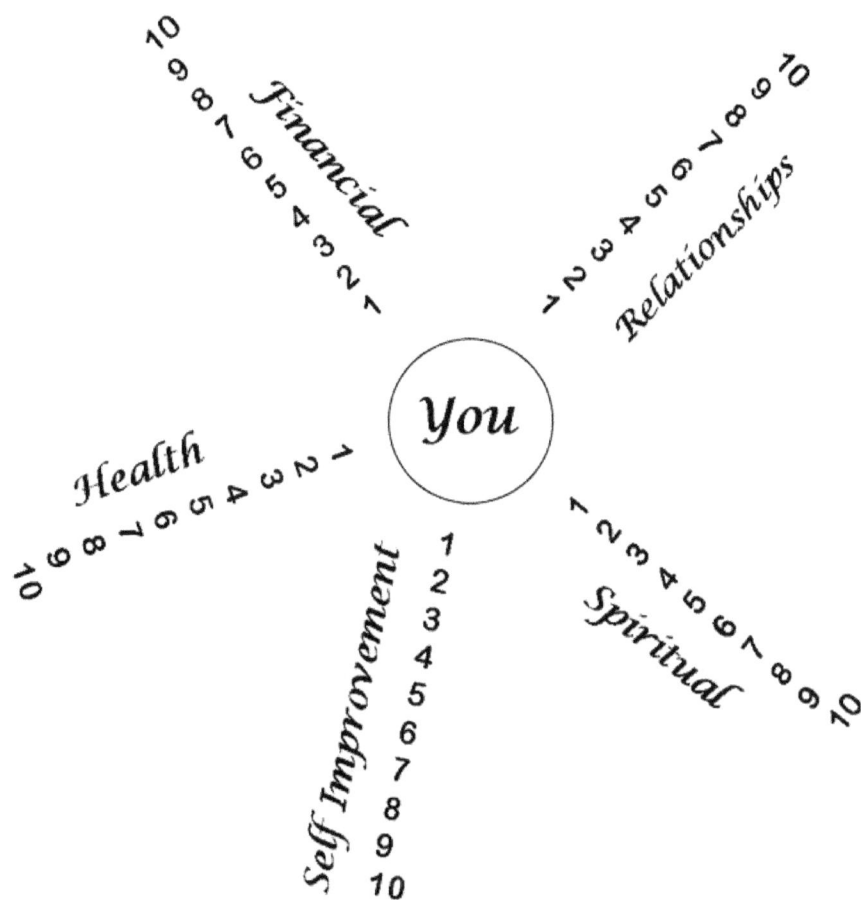

How well rounded is your life?

In each area of life, circle the number that best describes where you feel you are. One being the farthest from your best and ten stating there is no room for improvement. Now connect the numbers and make a circle.

How bumpy is your circle?

How well rounded are you? Is your life in balance or are you rolling down the road of life with a flat tire? Most people's lives are not in perfect balance; I know I am constantly working on mine!

When you are ready to write down your dreams, ponder the areas of your life that may need some extra attention and set a goal in that area. Do this exercise a couple of times each year to help you keep your life in balance. Extra forms are in the back of this guide.

A balanced life is a fulfilling life

Chapter Five

Start Today

Reach For Your Dreams

"You will never win, if you never begin."
Helen Rowland

One of the most difficult things about dream achievement is simply getting started. When you *do* start and you take your first step, the momentum begins!

When should *you* start?

- Now
- Today
- Right this minute
- Don't wait until tomorrow

Let's get started!

❧ Congratulations!
Reading this guide is your first step
to dream achievement. Don't dither;
keep your momentum going! ❧

Part II

Setting the Goal

"Success is a state of mind. If you want success,
start thinking of yourself as a success."
Dr. Joyce Brothers

Winners strategize

This is where you set yourself apart from the average person

Chapter Six

Clarifying Your Dreams and Goals

"To achieve, you need thought.
You have to know what you are doing and that's real power."
Ayn Rand

Being extremely clear on what is important to you gives your dreams and goals power, and with power you will be unstoppable. When you know what each dream's purpose is, then you have a reason to pursue that dream.

This first exercise is on clarity and it will help you identify the *why* of each dream.

I want you to fully understand clarity before you do the exercise, so please read through these brief definitions:

What is clarity of a dream?

- When you have a crystal clear vision of what you want
- When you know the purpose of your dream
- When you are able to visualize yourself reaching your dream
- When you know the dream is your own, not someone else's

Why is clarity important?

- When you know *exactly* what you want, you will have a burning desire to overcome all obstacles to achieve your dream
- When the goal is your own, it will have an exclusive purpose, special to you, creating motivation and enthusiasm
- You will believe in yourself and in your ability to achieve that dream
- Your goals will be in alignment with your values
- You will be excited with each action step you take

The following exercise (form on next page) will help you have a clearer picture on your dreams.

Part I.   Write down 5 things you want to achieve.

Examples: Be debt free
               Lose 20 pounds
               Have a better relationship with……
               Be my own boss
               Send my children to college

Part II. Now write down why you want to achieve these dreams, the purpose.

Examples: So I can stop worrying
               To feel healthier
               I will be happier
               I can take time off and spend more time with my family
               So they can have a good career

List five dreams.

_____

_____

_____

_____

_____

What is your purpose for each dream?

_____

_____

_____

_____

_____

Chapter Seven

Writing Your Dreams and Goals

"There is no chance, no destiny, no fate that can circumvent
or hinder or control the firm resolve of a determined soul."
Ella Wheeler Wilcox

Now that you have clarity on your dreams, the next step is to write them down using the D R E A M S criteria and explore the possible obstacles and solutions for each.

The steps to setting effective goals are outlined in this chapter, and the *My Dream* forms are provided at the end of the chapter. Please read through the full chapter before you begin to fill out the *My Dream* form so you have a better understanding of the full process.

Step One: Writing the Dream

Choose one of the dreams you wrote down in the last exercise. You are going to reword and rewrite that dream in a present and positive state, along with using the principles in the acronym **D R E A M S**.

A present and positive state is best described as:

- Written as if you have already achieved the goal
- Written in first person
- Written with positive verbiage

Examples: I am debt free and I make _____ per month.
I am healthy and I weigh 140 pounds.
I go on a date every Friday night with _____.
My company's name is _____ and we market
_____. Our annual revenue is _____.
My children attend _____ University.

It is important to write your goal using positive verbiage and then in present state because:

- It brings the fine points of your dream into focus
- Your mind believes what you say, so say it out loud and when you say it, your mind *will* believe it
- You will be more aware of the opportunities that surround you
- Your dream works as an affirmation
- Both 'present and positive' are energizing

In conjunction with your goal being written in a present and positive manner, you will include the **D R E A M S** principle. The dreams principle ensures that your goal contains all of the criteria that make it achievable. The key to reaching your dreams is to write an *effective* goal; it's not just about putting words on paper.

This is the **D R E A M S** principle:

- **D**eadline: State a deadline; a completion date.
- **R**ealistic: *Can* it really happen? Is it logically possible?
- **E**xclusive: The dream is yours. It belongs to you.
- **A**ttainable: The dream must be achievable. Close your eyes and if you can't imagine yourself reaching the dream, it may not be attainable.
- **M**easurable: The goal must be measurable, meaning you can track or quantify your progress.
- **S**pecific: Your dream must be specific and you must know exactly, without any ambiguity, what the goal is.

Your goal *says* something and will have value and meaning to you when it is written properly.

Step Two: Benefits

Write down every benefit of your goal; benefits expose the true purpose of your dream. Some of what you write down here will be the same as when you clarified the purpose of your dream.
Below are a few of the reasons why is it important to write down the benefits of your goal:

- Benefits give you motivation and drive
- Benefits make you enthusiastic
- Benefits help you stay on task and focus intensely on the end result
- Benefits give you a reason and a purpose to keep going
- You know exactly 'why' you are working toward your dream

Step Three: Obstacles

In this step, you are going to write down every obstacle that you believe you could encounter in reaching your dream.

Obstacles are setbacks and/or difficulties that you may have to overcome to reach your goal. When you are pondering what obstacles you may encounter, think about physical obstacles, such as lack of money or time constraints. Also consider mental obstacles, such as any fear or doubt that you may need to overcome.

Some of the reasons for this step are:

- Being ready for obstacles make them appear smaller and easier to conquer
- Preparing for possible setbacks will reduce the number of future surprises
- You will have more time for strategic planning
- It will help minimize or eliminate possible frustration in the future
- Recognizing your obstacles in advance gives you a precise focus
- You will be ready to brush off any doubt that you may encounter

Don't skip over any obstacles because you think it won't happen to you; write it down so if it does, you are ready to take on the world!

Step Four: Solutions

In this step, you become a problem-solver and create ways around the obstacles. These stumbling blocks are perfect opportunities for growth. You will grow stronger and more capable with each obstacle you overcome.

Below are some of the main reasons you want to think through and write down your solutions:

- You will be prepared to take action on predetermined obstacles
- You will not have any excuses for procrastination
- It will help minimize future frustration
- You will not become overwhelmed at the first sign of complications
- You will be more likely to take on any obstacles that you didn't foresee and you will be able keep moving forward

The obstacles that you may face, and you *will* conquer, will set you apart from others who get frustrated and just give up.

Step Five: Major Action Items

In this step, take the time to consider what major action items you will need to act upon to achieve your dreams. Some goals may only have a couple of smaller steps, while larger goals will require many major items. Don't be concerned here with every step you will need to take, just the major steps. In the following chapters, you will have the opportunity to break down large goals into milestones and then even further on the form *Dream Steps* (to-do list).

Write down the major things you will need to do, know and obtain to achieve your dream. Some questions to ask yourself are:

- What do I need to do?
- Who do I need to know?
- What do I need to learn?
- What do I need to obtain?

These are the main reasons you are writing down your action steps:

- Written and planned (more on planning in chapter 11) action steps eliminate procrastination
- You will know precisely what you need to do to achieve your dream
- You will know what additional skills you may need to acquire
- You will know what contacts you will need to make
- You will be able to create an effective plan to get you to your dream

Step Six: Reward

Write a reward, and make it a personal reward for your efforts and for the obstacles you may have to overcome. This is a reward over and above the benefits of reaching the dream. This reward gives you additional incentive to reach your goal.

Below are some additional reasons to have a reward:

- Rewards give you extra motivation
- Rewards make your journey feel worthwhile
- Rewards allow you to involve your family in your successes
- Rewards allow you to share something with others who have been supportive

Some simple ideas for rewards would be your favorite dessert, time with your family, a date, a day off, or simply a nice long, soothing bath!

Now, it's time to write a dream on the *My Dream* form. Promise yourself 10 minutes of time each day until your most important dreams are written in the D R E A M S format.

➤ IMPORTANT ◄

Oftentimes you will have a dream that, when you achieve it, your other goals will be easier to attain.

When you are choosing the goal to begin with, take this fact into consideration.

[On the following pages you will find some blank My Dream forms. Write your most important dream first.]

Sample

My Dream: *(positive and present tense)*

I weigh 140 pounds and as a result I feel great every morning and I am able

to do the physical things that I enjoy doing!

Deadline ☒ Realistic ☒ Exclusive ☒ Attainable ☒ Measurable ☒ Specific ☒

Deadline Date: December 31, year

Benefits from Achieving this Goal:

I will fit into my clothes comfortably, I will not be as tired, My back will not ache

I will be able to hike with ease and do the active things I love to do.

Possible Obstacles:

Friends inviting me to lunch, Holiday Dinners, Too busy to exercise,

sore muscles

Possible Solutions:

Share goal with family and ask for support from them, Eat every item I love

but take smaller portions,   eat slower and refuse second helpings, Get up

$\frac{1}{2}$ hour earlier each morning to exercise, Find a physical activity buddy

Major Action Items:

Eat slower and have smaller portions, Exercise 30 minutes 5 times per week

Weigh myself every other day, Drink more water

Reward(s)   Buy new clothes that fit!

My Dream: (positive and present tense)

_____

_____

_____

Deadline ☐ Realistic ☐ Exclusive ☐ Attainable ☐ Measurable ☐ Specific ☐

Deadline Date:

_____

Benefits from Achieving this Goal:

_____

_____

_____

Possible Obstacles:

_____

_____

_____

Possible Solutions:

_____

_____

_____

Major Action Items:

_____

_____

_____

_____

Reward(s)

_____

My Dream: (positive and present tense)

_____

_____

_____

Deadline ☐ Realistic ☐ Exclusive ☐ Attainable ☐ Measurable ☐ Specific ☐

Deadline Date:

_____

Benefits from Achieving this Goal:

_____

_____

_____

Possible Obstacles:

_____

_____

_____

Possible Solutions:

_____

_____

_____

Major Action Items:

_____

_____

_____

_____

Reward(s)

Congratulations! With just one of your dreams on paper, you have made more progress toward that dream than the majority of adults have made toward any one of their dreams.

You are more likely to achieve your dreams when you have a written and well thought out plan

Chapter Eight

Breaking Your Big Dreams

Into Smaller, Tangible Dreams

Be faithful in small things because it is in
them that your strength lies.
Mother Teresa

When you have a big dream, it works best to break it up into smaller dreams, creating smaller goals within your big dream.   It's more difficult to put an effective plan in place for a very large dream because of the amount of steps and the time frame it may demand.

When you create smaller goals, which we will call milestones, you will have goals that are within reach, that keep you motivated and on task to reach your larger dream. With milestone goals written in the **D R E A M S** format, your plan can be scheduled on a current calendar and you can create distinct, actionable steps.

A dream that is very large or long term may, at times, seem so far away that you lose sight of your dream and lose the drive to reach it. With milestone goals, you will achieve smaller goals often, keeping you motivated, *and* you will be earning rewards on a regular basis!

To put this concept into perspective, let's use the example of preparing to run a full marathon. You could break your big goal up into mileage increments, or you could start with shorter races such as a 5k, and then a 10k, creating smaller milestones. With a smaller goal, your dreams will be within touch and your motivation will remain high. You will reach your milestone goals in your quest for the bigger dream, the full marathon!

Below are reasons why you should break up large dreams:

- It is easier to reach a number of smaller dreams
- It allows you to focus on current action steps
- Reaching milestone goals invigorate and inspire you
- Milestone goals aid in easy measurement of your progress
- When a goal is too far away, you won't feel the same inner motivation as you will when your dream, or milestone, is within reach

To simplify this task, here are step-by-step instructions for creating milestone goals:

1. Working with your big dream, break it into chunks, each chunk being a milestone goal
2. Write the milestone goal on a *My Dream* form using the **D R E A M S** format
3. This *is* your goal; it's the one you will start with
4. When you have success, *and you will*, write out your next milestone goal
5. Keep the successes and the rewards coming by using milestone goals until you reach your BIG DREAM!

Realize that the large or long term goal may need to be modified during your progress; that is okay! Rewrite it and change anything you must, including the deadline date. Be open to changes, keep up your momentum and do not give up!

❦ Big Dreams are best broken up into smaller tangible dreams ❧

Chapter Nine

Dream Steps

"Determination and perseverance move the world;
thinking that others will do it for you is a sure way to fail."
Marva Collins

Your dreams are on paper and you know why you want to achieve your dreams. You know what obstacles you may have to overcome and you have designed a plan to tackle them by writing your solutions. You have also identified the major action items you are going to have to act upon to achieve your dreams.

Next you are going to use the *Dreams Steps* form, which you will find at the end of this chapter. Very simply, *Dream Steps* is your to-do list. This list is an ever-changing list and you are constantly adding things to the list and crossing items off the list as you complete them. *Dream Steps* is not limited to the things you need to accomplish for your dreams; it includes *everything* you need to do, including all personal and everyday items.

Look at your major action items and start writing down *everything* that you need to do to accomplish these items. Place a completion date on your tasks, taking into consideration the completion dates of your dreams. You may not be able to add a completion date to every to-do item right away but as you get closer to your goal, you can add that date. Not everything you put on your list, especially personal *want*-to-do's, will need to have a completion date.

The *Dream Steps* list will be referenced when you are planning your days (planning in chapter 11).

Remember, use just one list for everything, personal and dream steps, to keep you organized. There is no need for more than one list and never a need for more than one calendar or organizer.

How to use your *Dream Steps* list effectively:

In the priority column use this numbering system so you can easily identify your most important and urgent tasks:

> 1 = Urgent and both important and not important, dream step and personal, must be scheduled right away

> 2 = Not urgent but important, dream step and personal, must be done in a timely manner

> 3 = Not urgent and not important, usually personal, something you *want* to get done (these will pile up quickly, so do try to schedule these items sporadically throughout the month)

Be sure to add a completion date to the time sensitive items.

Again, this is the list you will use when you are planning your days.

*Knowing what action steps you must take
is key to reaching your dreams*

Dream Steps

Priority	To-Do	Completion Date

Dream Steps

Priority	To-Do	Completion Date

PART III

TAKING ACTION

AND

STAYING MOTIVATED

*To make big steps, you've got to take action
yourself and not listen to other people.*
Juliana Hatfield

Achievers take Action

This is where your dreams start to transpire

Chapter Ten

Dream Weaving

Making a Commitment to Yourself

We all have our own life to pursue, our own kind of dream to be weaving.
And we all have some power to make wishes come true,
as long as we keep believing.
Louisa May Alcott

Before I go any further, I want to get you committed. I want you to commit, right now, to *Dream Weaving* every day. It only takes 10 minutes and it keeps your dreams alive, motivates you, and actually helps you create more time.

> *That's right, after your dreams are written down on the My Dream form, it takes only 10 minutes each day to keep your dreams from fading away!*

Dream Weaving broken down:

<u>In the Morning</u>

Affirmations/incantation	1 minute	(chapter 12)
Read your dreams (just the *dream* itself)	2 minutes	(*My Dream* form)
Look at your dream board	1 minute	(chapter 13)
Glance at your planner	1 minute	(chapter 11)

<u>In the Evening:</u>

Plan your next day	5 minutes	(chapter 11)

Commit to *Dream Weaving* every day; it is one of the most important things you can do to help you achieve your dreams.

When you Dream Weave, you will find yourself using your time more efficiently, getting more done in less time, and *that* is one of the best ways to find time for your dreams.

∽ *Make a commitment to yourself* ∾

[Make a commitment to yourself.
Sign the following completed Commitment to Myself certificate
or use the blank commitment form and write your own unique
commitments to yourself and sign it.

Hang it where you and others will see it every day.
Your family is often your biggest source of support and inspiration.]

Commitment
To Myself

I commit to pursue my dreams by taking control of my life and making time for dream achievement.

I commit to clarify my goals and write them down.

I commit to Dream Weave every day.

I commit to take at least one action step each day, no matter how small.

I believe in myself and my dreams.

My dreams will become reality.

_____

Signature

_____

Date

Commitment To Myself

_____

_____

_____

_____

_____

_____

_____

_____
Signature

_____
Date

Chapter Eleven

Planning and Time Management

Plan your work for today and every day,
then work your plan.
Margaret Thatcher

Planning is crucial; it is another key to achieving your dreams. In this chapter, you will learn how to plan, and you will find that planning is a time creation tool.

Your game board is completely set up now and it is time to play the game. You must strategize and plan, then physically make your move. Planning and taking action is how you win; how you achieve your dreams.

With your next day planned, you will take action and follow your schedule. You will find yourself being *more productive* because you know exactly what you must accomplish and when. In turn, you will actually be creating extra time in your day, time that you can put toward your dreams. Beginning today, you will plan and schedule your next day.

Before I move onto the instructional part about planning, I want to share a multitude of reasons why planning is so important:

- You will be more productive
- Planning fine tunes your focus
- You will be more organized
- You won't feel overwhelmed
- You will reach your dreams more easily and sooner than you imagined
- Every morning, you will be enthusiastic because you know exactly what steps need to be done to get you closer to your dream
- You won't forget personal appointments

- You will eliminate double booking important dates and reduce the frustration of cancellations
- When you know that all of your important tasks are scheduled to be done, and they *will* get done, you can focus on the task at hand
- Planning takes the guesswork out of each day
    - Example: You schedule physical activity at 6:00 a.m. and when you wake up, you don't lie in bed thinking "Well, should I get up and do some physical activity?" No! You say "It's time to get up and do some physical activity because I know this is part of my health goal and I will feel better all day because of it!"
- You will create more time for yourself and your goals
    - It is said that for every 1minute of planning, you will save approximately 10 minutes of time in the execution of your tasks. This concept alone should motivate you to plan your day. This adds up to approximately 5 extra hours of time each week. This time 'belongs' to you! Take it; it's yours!

The amount of time you schedule for your action steps is your decision and may change daily. My suggestion here is that you schedule *at least* one action step toward your dreams, even if it is making just one call, writing one sentence, or researching one thing that you need to know, on an otherwise busy day.

Generally, the amount of time you schedule for your dreams should be in direct correlation to the deadline dates on your dreams. Without a deadline that you are serious about, a three month goal may *never* get accomplished.

If you devote just 15 minutes of each day to taking small steps toward your dreams, you will yield over 100 minutes each week! And that's on top of the time you will reap because you are more efficient due to planning.

For me, the simplest way to plan is to look at my month and block out time for my dreams. I won't schedule any specific activities in those time blocks unless I have a large project that must be completed or started.

On Sunday evening, I will look at the upcoming weekly calendar and my Dream Steps list. I will note any appointments and schedule the #1 and #2 priority items that need to be done in that week.

Then each evening, I will add any other items to the following day that have come up and need to be done.

Broken down, the following is an excellent way to create productive days. Have a plan for every day, whether you plan daily or weekly.

- Monthly

    - Look at your upcoming month and block out all discretionary time where you will say NO to everything else. This is the time that you can make an appointment with yourself to work on your dreams
    - Look at your dreams and write down any large tasks that must be accomplished throughout the month. Stay on track with your goal completion dates and schedule time to tackle those tasks

- Weekly

    - View your week for any appointments or scheduled events
    - Schedule anything you can from your *Dream Steps* list now

- Daily

    - Each night before you go to bed, plan your next day, hour by hour
        - o Note: If you are unable to plan in the evening, plan your day first thing when you wake up
        - o Note: If planning daily doesn't work for you, then plan the full week on Saturday or Sunday, but be sure to plan *each* day out fully

Please read this small section. *These tips will help you create a more efficient and organized planning system:*

- Have only **one** planner, use what works best for you: electronic planner, manual planner, or calendar of your choice
- Use your *Dream Steps* list consistently, writing **every task** that you need to complete and continually add to it. Writing these to-dos down will relieve the stress of having to think "Don't forget to….."
    - Use this list to schedule at least one action step toward your dreams every day (no matter how small)
- When you do not have access to your planner, do not write notes or appointments on 'floating papers.' They tend to do a disappearing act, never to be seen again. Instead keep a small notebook handy, one you can carry with you
- At the end of each day, straighten and clear your desk or work area so you will start your next day off organized. This can save as much as 15 to 30 minutes of time the next morning because you can jump right into what needs to be accomplished
- Look at your planner every evening before you go to bed

Make it a habit (habits – chapter 16) to plan every day, part of your commitment to *Dream Weave*, and watch your life positively change!

✍ *Be conscientious of what you spend your time on!* ✍

Chapter Twelve

Affirmations and Incantations

"Never give up on your dreams...Perseverance is all important.
If you don't have the desire and the belief in yourself to keep trying
after you've been told you should quit, you'll never make it."
Tawni O'Dell

There is only a slight difference between affirmations and incantations. Both generate positive thought and give you inspiration, but they have a different purpose.

❖ Affirmations are brief and positive statements. Use affirmations to positively improve your thoughts and beliefs.

❖ Incantations are more powerful and thought provoking, positive statements. Use an incantation to have a commanding start to your day or to fill you full of inspiration any time during the day.

Affirmations

When you say your affirmations, say them out loud and with belief.

Examples of affirmations:

I choose to be happy and healthy.
I am extremely fortunate because I am loved by those around me.
I am intelligent.
I am excited about life and reaching my dreams.
I am healthy and I love healthy food.
I am the perfect weight for me.
I am at peace with myself.
I believe in myself.

I am capable of doing the things that will lead me to my dreams.
I plan each day and complete that plan without hesitation.
I love my job.
I love my husband.
I LOVE LIFE!

Incantations

Morning incantations will give you a positive and powerful start to your day. Say them out loud, in a commanding manner, and with all the energy you can muster.

I want to share with you that each morning when I say my incantation, I look at myself in the mirror, then I smile and go for it! I know this sounds a bit silly but it really works. It's the mirror that adds the extra punch; it is the visualization, the 'seeing' of yourself proclaiming your beliefs. I feel so energized after I say it!

I'll share another secret; if I am having a day that is not going as planned, I find the closest mirror and say an incantation that is appropriate for the moment. Incantations will help you get through rough moments and even sad times.

Examples of morning incantations

I will win because I have a purpose and that makes me enthusiastic!
I am happy, healthy and wealthy!
Today is going to be a great day because I _____
And as a result I _____!

I enjoy waking up each morning at _____ a.m. because I know it creates the time to get the things done that will lead me toward the achievement of my dreams. I had plenty of sleep and I feel great! I will do the most important step toward reaching my goal of _____ first, before anything else, because that is what is truly important to me.

. . . .

I am in control of my actions and I choose to take steps toward my dreams every day. I am in charge of my life and I will be persistent until my dream
is reached. I choose to win!

I love the following example of an evening incantation. It helps me sleep well.

I don't say it in the mirror because I don't need to be energized right now. I say it quietly to myself because it is time to wind down and get the best rest possible so I can be at my best the next day. Try it tonight!

Example of an evening incantation:

I am waking up at _____ a.m. in the morning because I know it creates the time to get the things done that will lead toward the achievement of my goals. I am so excited about reaching my goal of _____! I am going to bed at _____ p.m. and I will feel great tomorrow because _____ hours is plenty of sleep for me to feel great and to be able to achieve what is truly important to me.

. . . .

I know I have done my best today and I am satisfied with that. I have scheduled everything that is important for tomorrow, so I have no worries.

It is time to rest and get some sleep and when I wake up, I will be refreshed and ready to start the new day.

Modify these or create your own, but say affirmations and incantations every day. They will make your day more rewarding and worthwhile.

Optimism positively changes your life

Chapter Thirteen

Visualization

"People create their own questions because they are afraid to look straight. All you have to do is look straight and see the road, and when you see it, don't sit looking at it – walk."
Ayn Rand

Visualization is another key factor in staying motivated. Your mind activates every time you 'see' your dream.

Using visualization is easy. Simply create a *dream board* and hang it where you will see it regularly. A *dream board* is a collage of your dreams. Place pictures and/or words of your dreams on this board.

To build your dream board you will need:

> Poster board
> Pictures or words of your dreams
> Glue or tape

Create a collage of your dreams.

Hang your dream board next to your mirror, bed, in your shower using a large waterproof zipper bag, or in your work area and look at it often.

I have 3 dream boards around my home. My larger poster dream board is in my shower. The other two are smaller dream boards that I printed from my computer on photo paper and they hang at my desk and by my bed.

Visualization and planning are the best tools I have found and if you use both of these techniques, you will reach your dreams!

See what you desire and
go after what you see

Part IV

A Compilation of Valuable Information and Useful Tips

"We are hungry for more;
if we do not consciously pursue the More,
we create less for ourselves
and make it more difficult to experience More in life."
- Judith Wright

In this section, I am going to share a variety of tips and ideas, on a multitude of different topics. The purpose for this section is to provide information that will compliment the goal setting process and supply other basic tips that you can use in your daily routine to make your life a bit easier.

You may notice that many of the topics you read have some of the same tips and/or solutions. You will also find that the activities you do in your 10 minutes of *Dream Weaving*, will benefit you in most areas of life.

Dream Weaving is one of the most valuable tools you will use in your daily life.

Chapter Fourteen

Finding and Creating Time

*"You will find the time to accomplish the things
that are truly important to you."*
Shanna Beaman

"My life is so hectic! Where do I find more time?"

Generally, it is quite easy to make time for the urgent and necessary things in life.

Finding time for the non-urgent things seems to be an obstacle in most women's lives. Since most dreams seem to fall into this category, I am dedicating this chapter to helping you find time for your dreams.

Below are some ideas that may work for you:

- Recognize your discretionary time and schedule an appointment with yourself, blocking out that time slot right away
- Learn how to say "No" to requests and offers that do not benefit you
  - A nice way to decline an offer is to say "I'm sorry. I already have plans for that time."
- Do not take on extra tasks that take you further from your goals, and agree to only the necessary favors for others
  - Ask yourself this phrase "Will this take me closer to or farther away from my dream?"
- Plan a regularly scheduled day and time with a babysitter
- Plan a consistent babysitting trade schedule with someone you trust
- Plan a daily or weekly 'movie time' for your children
- Substitute your TV time for dream achievement time

- Unsubscribe to unnecessary emails and be conscious of your time on the web
- Take a 15, maybe 30 minute 'bathroom break,' with the door locked, and do some planning, writing, or phone calls (not necessarily in the bathroom)
- Consolidate like tasks and complete them simultaneously or consecutively
- When you work (inside or outside your home), take advantage of your lunchtime break and any other breaks that you are offered
  - Don't feel guilty, this time is *yours,* you have earned it
  - When you plan your day, schedule what you will accomplish during each break
    o Make a call
    o Plan your next day
    o Complete an action step
    o Run an errand during this limited span of time to free up a larger block of time later for 'dream achievement'
- Share your goals with your husband, children and others who are close to you so they will be more respectful of your time
  - Keep your family focused and motivated to respect your time by hanging up pictures of their reward; having two or more rewards for one goal is not against the rules, so feel free to add rewards when needed; everyone involved needs motivation
- Use your opportunity clock (metaphor for alarm clock) and get up one hour earlier
  - Note: When you wake up 1 hour earlier and devote this full hour to your dreams, you will gain 7 hours each week which is almost 1 full working day. *Each year you will accumulate approximately 50 extra 8 hour dream achievement days!*
- If you are more productive at night, go to bed one hour later instead of getting up early; the same concept in the note above applies here
- Get better sleep
  - Plan your next day in the evening so your mind is clear
  - Add anything new to your *Dream Steps* list

- Keep a notepad next to your bed to write down anything that may come to mind after you lie down
  - o Note: You can relax your mind when everything is written down and you will fall asleep faster
- Always carry a project with you that you can do on the run during any unexpected waiting time
- Keep a handheld recorder handy for ideas, thoughts, and reminders

The value of your time cannot be measured; taking advantage of 10 minute increments can make a big difference in your life, especially if those 10 minutes are planned and put to good use. Proper planning and effective time management actually snowballs and creates more free time.

➤IMPORTANT◄

By putting in some time and effort now, it will afford your family free time later and *that* free time will be the quality time that we all desire.

*Feel good, not guilty, about making time for **You** because, in the end, it will benefit the ones you love*

Chapter Fifteen

Solutions to Common Obstacles

*"I truly believe that we can overcome any hurdle that lies
before us and create the life we want to live.
I have seen it happen time and time again."*
Gillian Anderson

Recognizing obstacles is what sets the mediocre and the great apart.

Foreseeing and planning for possible obstacles is critical. When you put a tentative plan in place for your obstacles and you are faced with one, you can implement your plan of action and keep going. Facing an obstacle with your predetermined solution immediately knocks it down to a manageable size.

Not all obstacles may be predictable, so it is important to have tenacity to deal with the unforeseen ones. You will become stronger and more resilient with each triumph. Each new obstacle will bring about a learning and problem solving opportunity, so accept it as a chance for personal growth. Work out a solution and trounce on that obstacle!

Women experience many of the same obstacles in life and I want to share some solutions for these common obstacles:

- **Obstacle: Constant interruptions**

   Possible solutions:
   - Shut off your email and phone for a specified amount of time
   - Hang a 'Work Hours' sign on your door
   - Awaken before the rest of your family to work on *your* stuff

- Go somewhere that people do not have access to you
    - Library
    - Coffee Shop
    - Park
- Rent or borrow movies to entertain your children for short periods of time
- Find projects that your children can do on their own
- Offer a reward to your children when they allow a specific amount of quiet time for you
    - Note: Your children will be more cooperative when you ask them for help and let them know that at the end of their movie or project, you will be able to spend time with them. Then they can share their project with you or tell you what they liked about the movie. You will be amazed at how proud they are that they helped you.

- **Obstacle: Family expects more of your time**

Possible solutions:
- Share your dream and involve your family in the reward and the success
    - Example: "When I finish this project or reach this milestone, we will _____."
- Promise your undivided attention at a specific time or on a specific day
- Plan a break in your week and take a day to walk away from everything and do a fun, all day activity with the ones you love
- Let your family know that their patience is appreciated and that their involvement in your dream is making a big difference

- **Obstacle:** **You work all day, then you are a wife and a mother in the evening and you feel like you have no time for yourself or your dreams**

  Possible solutions:
  - Delegate some household chores
  - Before you go to bed, take 5 minutes to plan steps you can take the next day during your breaks and lunch time
  - Make sure you are taking every break offered to you at work – do not work through *your* time
  - Bring a lunch (save time and money) and take action steps during your lunch hour
  - Get to work before everyone else and work your plan; just 15 minutes/day = 75 minutes each week!
  - Use your opportunity clock and get up 30 minutes to 1 hour earlier

- **Obstacle:** **You are too tired to work on your goals**

  Possible solutions:
  - Plan your next day in the evening and you will get better sleep; it helps to clear your mind
  - Eat healthy foods
  - Take vitamin supplements
  - Drink more water to stay hydrated
  - Abstain from excessive alcohol
  - Revitalize yourself by reading your dreams
  - Energize yourself by saying your favorite incantation
  - Visualize your dreams and your rewards daily
  - Do regular physical activity

- **Obstacle: Your co-workers want you to go out to lunch**

    Possible solutions:
    - Share your dreams with trusted co-workers
    - Ask them to provide motivation and support
    - Ask your co-workers what their dreams are
    - Set aside one day each week and *do* go to lunch with them

- **Obstacle: You have a hard time saying "No" to other's requests**

    Possible solutions:
    - Have most of your discretionary time 'scheduled' for dreams
    - Learn to say "I am sorry, I already have plans for that time."
    - Ask yourself this phrase "Will this take me closer to or farther away from my dream?"
    - Always be aware of your time; time is one thing that you cannot recycle, so use it wisely

    If you want to agree to a request, don't forget to look at your calendar before committing; you do not want to double book something. Nothing good happens when you have to cancel an appointment that you have already scheduled.   Be mindful that an appointment that you have made for your dreams is just as important as any other. Just because the appointment is with *You,* do not take canceling it lightly.

Many successful people point out that their past obstacles and failures were their most valuable lessons. They credit what they learned from overcoming obstacles as a big part of their success.

Accept every obstacle as a learning experience and an opportunity to grow. Look for the good in everything; look for the lesson in every obstacle.

Obstacles will not be a barrier between you and your dreams

Chapter Sixteen

Changing Your Habits

"The universe has no favorites. Those who succeed
have created good habits and taken steps toward their goals."
Shanna Beaman

When you have habits that are not conducive to making you productive, it makes dream achievement burdensome. Bad habits make so many tasks seem like chores, but when you have good habits many of those 'chores' simply happen automatically and get done on autopilot.

With a small amount of initial time and discipline, you can actually create good habits that will require little effort to maintain. I have provided a form at the end of this chapter that will help you shape new habits and eliminate the habits that you don't want.

Many studies confirm that it only takes 21 consecutive days of effort to form a new habit. Commit to 21 days of conscious behavior, plan your attack against your bad habits and apply your energy toward creating strong, productive habits. Reaching your dreams will be considerably easier when innate behaviors work for you and not against you.

It is important to take some time to recognize which habits are holding you back and decide what new habits you need to create.

> ❧ *Create good habits and*
> *have the 'Do it now' attitude.* ☙

[Use the form on the next page
to help you change your habits]

Creating Good Habits

Write your new habit: _____

_____

What are the benefits of this new habit?_____

_____

What are the obstacles to creating this new habit?_____

_____

What are your solutions to overcome the obstacles?_____

_____

What are the action steps you must take?_____

_____

Deadline_____

Eliminating Bad Habits

Write your bad habit: _____

_____

What are the benefits of eliminating this habit?_____

_____

What are the obstacles to overcoming this habit?_____

_____

What are your solutions to overcome the obstacles?_____

_____

What are the action steps you must take?_____

_____

Deadline_____

Chapter Seventeen

Commitment and Persistence

*"When I thought I couldn't go on, I forced myself to keep going.
My success is based on persistence, not luck."*
Estee Lauder

Your success relies heavily upon unwavering determination and persistence. You can achieve your dreams, your passions, and your desires with a good attitude, smart work, and persistence.

Below are ideas that may help you to be more persistent:

- Look at your dream board and visualize what it is going to feel like when you achieve those dreams
- Read your goals every day
- Have a plan and work it every day
- Rewrite your plan when it isn't working for you
- Create new habits
- Rid yourself of the habits that hold you back
- Don't be afraid of change
- Kick fear out of your life
- Work toward your well deserved rewards
- Surround yourself with successful people
- Don't listen to others who say "just quit" or "you'll never do that"
- Never stop with the first no
- Be willing to pay the price
- Be willing to put unimportant things on hold
- Fill your vocabulary with positive words (chapter 21)
- Figure out *exactly* what you want to accomplish
- Write your goals using the D R E A M S guidelines
- Write down your obstacles
- Write down your solutions to overcome those obstacles
- Write down every step you must take
- Believe in yourself

Do you ever wonder why some people are not persistent? These are some of the reasons I believe some individuals lack the fine quality of perseverance:

- They don't have discipline and tenacity
- They are not willing to pay the price
- They don't set clearly defined goals
- They refuse to put other things on hold
- They are 'ruled' by and don't know how to overcome obstacles
- They have not built a solid foundation for good habits

> Thomas J. Stanley, author of The Millionaire Mind, surveyed hundreds of millionaires and he found that most of the respondents did not inherit their money, go to Ivy League Colleges, nor were they at the top of their class throughout school. Most of these individuals attribute their fortunes to hard work, persistence and attitude.

When times get tough and the task at hand is grueling, keep going! Never give up!

Chapter Eighteen

Eliminate Procrastination

"A year from now you may wish you had started today."
Karen Lamb

Achieving your dreams takes action; achievers take action. When you procrastinate tasks get put off, and oftentimes, taking action on your *Dream Steps* never happen. If you don't take action, you will not experience your dreams. Dreams do not seek you, you seek dreams.

When procrastination is an issue, you must to take steps toward changing your behavior. Don't let procrastination be in charge of your life; *Dream Weave* every day!

Things you can do to stop procrastinating:

- Stop thinking about it; just do it
- Have a sense of urgency
- Break bad habits
- Be disciplined
- Believe in yourself
- Plan your next day, hour by hour, the evening before
- Do the item that will yield the most results first, when possible
- Stay focused on one task until it is done; don't get sidetracked
- Make one *Dream Steps* list and update it regularly
- Use one calendar or scheduler
- Allow fun time only after you complete your most important task of the day
- Learn to say "No" to things that hinder dream achievement

- Schedule blocks of uninterrupted time regularly in which to take action on your dreams
- Commit to not checking email, unless applicable, during scheduled uninterrupted time
- Commit to turning your phone off during scheduled uninterrupted time
- Hold yourself accountable
- Partner up with someone who will hold you accountable
- Report your progress (and failures) to someone else
- Let your family know what you are doing and ask for their support
- Give yourself deadlines (time and date) to finish a project
- Set your desk up to be conducive to productive work
- Require yourself to finish at least one action step before going to bed
- Take a break for rejuvenation, but decide on a specific task to complete after your break
- Build momentum by getting one, then two, then three things done
- Break a large project into bite size, manageable pieces
- Get started on a project by doing the easiest part first; build momentum from there
- Face your fears; most fears can be overcome with a plan
- Identify your obstacles and plan your strategy
- Finish a task before you start on a new one
- Get organized
- Make your tasks as fun as possible
- Reward yourself and others
- Don't over schedule your days
- Create a routine and plan recurring tasks at the same time every day
- Say affirmations/incantations every day
- Read and visualize your dreams

If you are a perfectionist, this may be one reason for your procrastination. Things are rarely going to be perfect, so step outside of your comfort zone and get started. Maintain high standards but don't expect perfection.

*No time is better than right now;
Get started on your dreams*

Chapter Nineteen

Believe In Yourself

Focus more on your desire than on your doubt, and the dream will take care of itself. You may be surprised at how easily this happens. Your doubts are not as powerful as your desires, unless you make them so."
Marcia Wieder

We haven't discussed how important it is to believe in yourself. You are the only person who has control over your thoughts. You must empower yourself to think positive thoughts about yourself and your abilities. In order to reach your dreams, you must believe in yourself.

It is essential to focus on your dreams and not your doubts. You can be, do and have the things you want in life…and you deserve it. What you think and say will change how you feel. Your life and your attitude will improve when you let go of limiting beliefs.

Below are examples of how to reshape your thoughts, giving you the power to enrich your life.

Limiting Belief	vs.	Empowering Belief
I don't have the time.	to	I have plenty of time to do the things that are truly important to me.
I am depressed.	to	I have total control over how I feel every day; I choose to be happy.
I'm not smart enough.	to	I am intelligent and I can learn anything that I desire.
It's too late to start.	to	I am starting today or It's never too late to start.
It's a bad habit that I can't kick.	to	I am in control of my habits.

I don't deserve _____.	to	I am a good person and I always put my best foot forward; I deserve _____.
I can't depend on others.	to	I am capable and I depend on myself.
I am selfish wanting more; I should be happy with what I have.	to	It is not selfish to want more. I deserve to have the things in life that I strive for, and with the personal growth I will experience, I will be able to give more to others.

Below are tips and things you can do to help you overcome limiting beliefs:

- Say positive affirmations daily
- Take baby steps outside of your comfort zone
- Don't speak or think negative words (chapter 21)
- Commit to saying only positive, uplifting things
- Empower yourself; take charge of your beliefs
- Always be at your best
- Believe that you can, *and you can,* do anything

Below are the things that I believe contribute to limiting beliefs:

- A fear of something
- A lack of confidence
- A past event
- A prior failure
- A past relationship (parent, teacher, spouse, etc)

If any of these things are holding you back from achieving your dreams, add them as obstacles on your *My Dream* form and figure out a solution for them.

Stay positive, focus on your dreams and know that I believe in you.

Limiting beliefs create an enormous burden on you emotionally, physically and spiritually. Surround yourself with people who believe in you and keep believing in yourself.

❧ *Focus on your dreams* ❧

*[Use the form on the next page
to help you create empowering beliefs.]*

Creating Empowering Beliefs

Write your limiting belief: _____
_____

Why do you believe this? _____
_____

What actions will you take to overcome this? _____
_____

How will you feel when you eliminate this limiting belief? _____
_____

Write your new empowering belief: _____
_____

Creating Empowering Beliefs

Write your limiting belief: _____
_____

Why do you believe this? _____
_____

What actions will you take to overcome this? _____
_____

How will you feel when you eliminate this limiting belief? _____
_____

Write your new empowering belief: _____
_____

Chapter Twenty

Having a Good Attitude

"If you don't like something, change it.
If you can't change it, change your attitude."
Maya Angelou

Have you ever had a bad experience with someone? When you stop and think about it; it is generally because one, or both, of you had a bad attitude.

When you have a good attitude and have an optimistic outlook on life, it will take you places that you never thought possible, allow you to meet people you never thought you would meet and present opportunities that you never thought you would have.

I know this because I have experienced many positive things in my life and I know it is because I am a true optimist. I love life and I share that love with others.

Not only will having a positive attitude change your life, it will change the lives of those around you.

There are more reasons than I can list here documenting why you should always have a good attitude. Here are just some of the reasons:

- Your life will flourish
- You will have more energy
- You will be more enthusiastic
- Every day is more fun
- You are more likely to believe in yourself
- You will accomplish more
- Relationships are better
- People will want to be around you

- People will want to help you
- More opportunities will present themselves
- You will go farther in life
-

Below are some things you can do that will help you to be more positive and have a good attitude:

- Think only good thoughts
- Greet everyone with a smile
- Say positive daily affirmations/incantations
- Have a daily inspiration quote sent to you via email
- Have an inspirational calendar
- Be thankful for everything you have
- Read and visualize your goals regularly
- Think about your rewards often
- Write down everything you are thankful for
- Say "Thank you for my wonderful life" every morning
- Tell someone "Thank you" for something they have done for you
- Appreciate your friends, family, and support groups
- Spend quality time with your family and friends
- Take action on a dream
- Close your eyes and plan out the perfect day and believe that you will experience that day soon

Your attitude plays a large part in how your life will unfold. If you are a pessimist and you think life is throwing things at you, stand back and look again. Take control of how you look at others and how you look at life in general. Put on a happy face, be kind to others, think positive thoughts and watch your life flourish.

You can be, do, and have anything you desire

Chapter Twenty-One

Eliminate Negative Thinking

Be an Optimist

*"If you realized how powerful your thoughts are,
you would never think a negative thought."*
Peace Pilgrim: Born Mildred Norman

Have you ever noticed that when you speak negatively about one thing, that negativity builds up and then bleeds into other parts of your life? The same concept works with positivity.

Stay away from derogatory words; speak kindly of others and positively about your situation. You will see your world change right before your eyes.

Consciously add positive words (see next page) to your vocabulary and replace words of failure with winning words (below).

Words of Failure	vs	Winning Words
Can't, Try		Can
Incapable		Capable
Won't Try, Maybe, Might		Will
If		When
Impossible		Possible
But		And
Someday, Never		Now or state a date

Positive Words

Wonderful Beautiful
Marvelous Kind
Positive Elegant Confident
Affirmative Love Creative
Great Splendid Assenting Exciting
Joyous Astounding Upbeat
Laugh Exceptional Remarkable
Worthy Breathtaking Charity Smart
Gleaming
Determined Incredible Gifted
Inspire Capable Happy Proud
Motivated Stunning Cheerful Radiant
Attractive Tremendous
Caring
Superb Magnificent Talented Terrific
Encouraging Smile
Excellent Gorgeous Yes
Stupendous Sensational
Awesome Extraordinary Leader
Fantastic Intelligent Brilliant
Admirable
Fabulous Energizing Amazing Inspired
Unstoppable Astonishing
Accomplish Commendable
Enterprising Outstanding
Unlimited Dazzling Likeable
Achieve

Created by Shanna Beaman at www.wordle.net

Chapter Twenty-Two

You *are* Remarkable

*"Fear of failure and fear of the unknown are always defeated by faith
Having faith in yourself, in the process of change, and in the next
direction that change sets will reveal your own inner core of steel."*
Georgette Mosbacher

I want to share some fun ways to help you create a more positive *You;* to help you identify your significance. It's nice when someone tells you how great you are, but sometimes you just need to see it for yourself.

The ideas below are activities you can do that will help you be more positive and believe more deeply in yourself; they will prove just how great you truly are.

Keep a 'ME' folder

Start a 'ME' folder and put every affirming memento in it. This is your private collection of gratification and you can pull it out whenever you need reassurance or a lift in your spirits.

How to:

1. Get a bright and fun folder
2. Place notes, letters, or emails from others mentioning ways you have influenced their lives in the folder
3. Put "Thank You" notes and cards that you have received in the folder
4. Place pictures that children have drawn for you, because you are special to them, in the folder
5. Put anything in this folder that is of significance to you
6. Look at this folder a regular basis

Remember to thank others and let them know when you think they are special by sending them something that, one day, they may put in their 'ME' folder.

Get re-acquainted with your past successes

When you are aware of your past successes, it will give you encouragement and motivate you to take action on new successes. You will see that you are capable of something spectacular!

How to:

1. Write down every success, no matter how small, that you have had since kindergarten.
2. Keep this in a place where you can review it regularly (In your 'ME' folder is be a good place!)
3. Add to this list each time you experience another success in your life.

Start a journal, writing good deeds and daily accomplishments

How to:

1. Get a nice journal that makes you feel good and that you enjoy writing in
2. Choose a time of the day that is good for you and jot down your daily accomplishments and don't be humble; you did it, you deserve it
3. Review your accomplishments whenever you need a pick-me-up

Recognize what is great about you

You have strengths and characteristics that make you unique and great. In life, you will be able to use these traits in a variety of ways as you encounter different situations.

On the next page, circle every word that describes you and don't be modest. After you are done, you will be more aware of the multitude of useful traits you have. Take advantage of these strengths and characteristics that you possess, and make them available to draw from when necessary.

What's Great About Me?

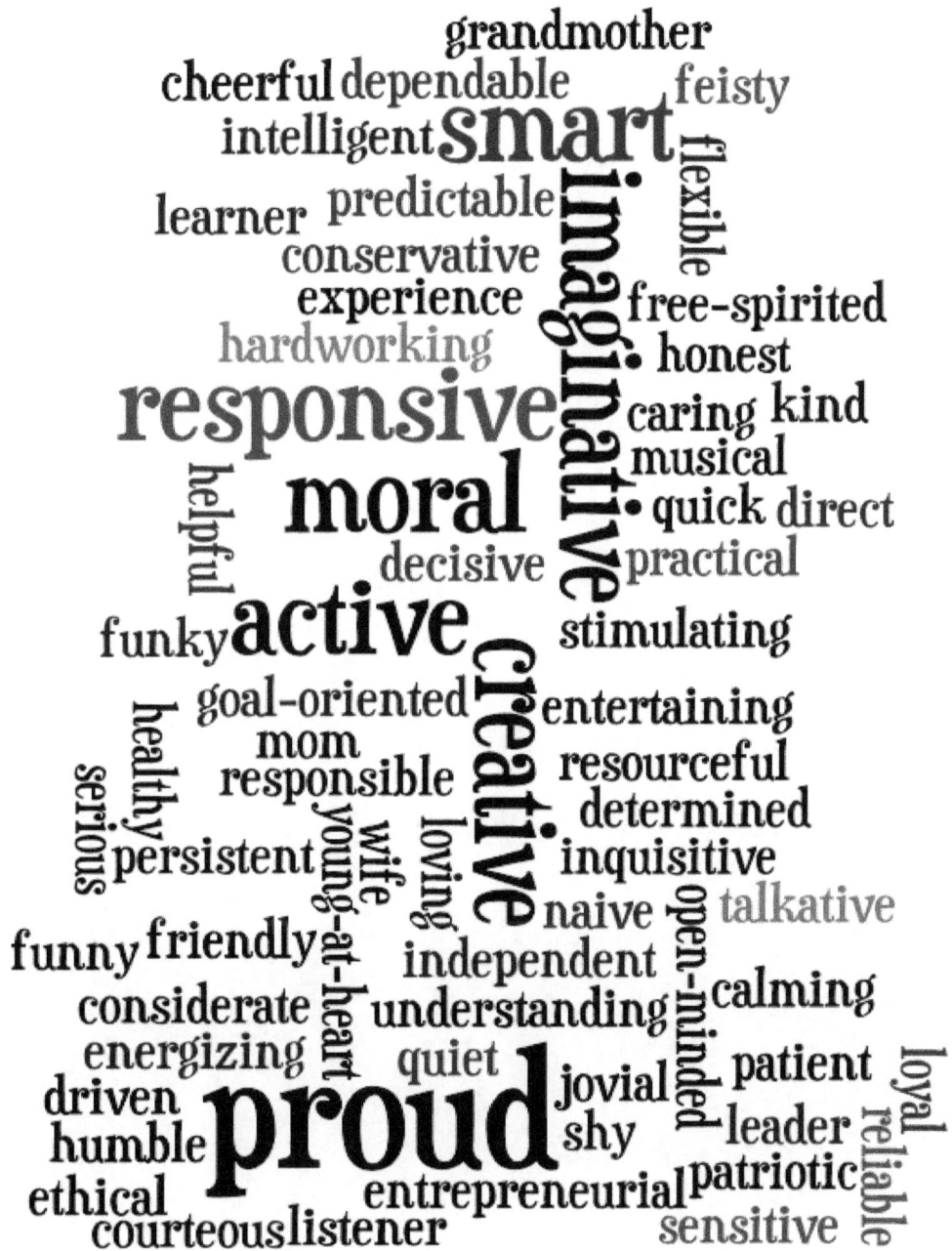

grandmother
cheerful dependable feisty
intelligent **smart** flexible
learner predictable imaginative
conservative
experience free-spirited
hardworking honest
responsive caring kind
musical
helpful **moral** quick direct
decisive practical
funky **active** stimulating
goal-oriented entertaining
healthy mom creative resourceful
serious responsible determined
persistent wife loving inquisitive
young-at-heart naive open-minded talkative
funny friendly independent calming
considerate understanding
energizing quiet patient loyal
driven **proud** jovial reliable
humble shy leader
ethical entrepreneurial patriotic
courteous listener sensitive

Created by Shanna Beaman at www.wordle.net

Chapter Twenty-Three

Gratitude

"Gratitude unlocks the fullness of life. It turns what we have into enough, and more. It turns denial into acceptance, chaos to order, confusion to clarity.
It can turn a meal into a feast, a house into a home, a stranger into a friend. Gratitude makes sense of our past, brings peace for today, and creates a vision for tomorrow."
Melody Beattie

Gratitude is an important key to happiness, success, and dream attainment.

When you are aware of everything that you have to be thankful for, it will help you enjoy life to a greater extent. Many people take for granted the beauty that surrounds them, the loved ones who are near them and even the fact that they woke up this morning. Since you are reading this guide, you can be thankful that you can read.

When you are thankful for what you have in your life, you will experience more pleasure every day.

Below are just a few of the things being grateful will do for you:

- You will be happier
- You will be enjoyable to be around
- People around you will be happier
- You will focus on your successes
- You won't focus on the negative
- You will worry less
- You will be less likely to fall into an unproductive state

Below are some ideas that may help bring more gratitude, more often, into your life:

- Start a gratitude journal
- Create a list of the things that you are thankful for
- Include a statement of thanks in your incantations/affirmations
- When reading your dreams each morning, be thankful that you have dreams
- Put a rock or piece of polished glass in your pocket and every time you see it or feel it, think of something you are grateful for
- Say thank you to others at every opportunity

When you are appreciative of the world around you, you will be putting yourself in a natural state of happiness.

Happiness begins with gratitude

Chapter Twenty-Four

Create Enthusiasm in Your Life

If you have enthusiasm, you have a very dynamic,
effective companion to travel with you on the road to Somewhere.
Loretta Young

Enthusiasm is the emotion that gives you the energy and the motivation that will propel you toward your dreams.

Enthusiasm is one of my 'given' attributes and it has proven itself to be a worthy companion throughout my life. Enthusiasm has taken me places and allowed me to build exceptional relationships, both in my career and in my personal life, that I would never have been able to experience without it.

Ways to create enthusiasm:

- Write down what a perfect day is for you – Now, go for it!
- Exchange ideas with other inspiring people
- Share goals with others who care and are supportive
- Say your most energetic incantation
- Read your goals every morning
- Write and rewrite your goals
- Be a student of self improvement
- Look at your dream board
- Put in your favorite motivational CD
- Watch a fun short You Tube or motivational video
- Join a club or group in your area of interest

Enthusiasm is a powerful tool for success. With passion for life, you will keep your dreams alive and being enthusiastic will help you get more done in less time.

With enthusiasm, you will be unstoppable!

Chapter Twenty-Five

Self Improvement

*"When we learn new behaviors and break through
to higher levels of consciousness and love,
we can fulfill the deeper spiritual hunger within".*
Judith Wright

Personal growth is an important key to happiness. Take every opportunity to develop yourself and make it a goal to learn something new every day, no matter how small.

Below are some ideas that will keep you learning:

- Use the internet
    - Take a web course/class
    - Attend free webinars
    - Participate in free phone calls
    - Request free items (newsletters, eBooks, audio)
    - Join a forum of interest
        - Note: When requesting freebies, unsubscribe to further communications if the information is not what you expected or if you are being overwhelmed with emails; excessive emails is a huge consumer of your valuable time
- Listen to inspirational, motivational and educational audio while you are driving, cleaning and/or do physical activity
    - Download from the internet
    - Check out audio from the library
    - Purchase new and used audio from websites/stores
- Check out your local library for free live classes on various subjects
- Take Continuing Education courses

- Join a local group
- Find a mentor
- Observe and learn from other successful people

Developing your knowledge isn't the only way to grow. Ask yourself questions like:

- How can I make this situation better?
- How can I make more money doing what I love?
- How can I be a better wife or mother?
- How can I show more love to others?
- What can I do to make the world a better place?

Decide what is important for you to improve upon without overwhelming yourself. Take the opportunity to improve your skills, your behavior, and your family life whenever you can.

What new skill or knowledge would take you closer to your dreams if you acquired it today?

Chapter Twenty-Six

Living a Healthy Lifestyle

*"I never could have achieved the success that I have
without setting physical activity and health goals."*
Bonnie Blair

The best way to stay healthy is to plan. Plan your family time, your meals, physical activity, and plan some alone time.

Create your plan before you become unhealthy and you are forced to take medications or do required exercise that you don't enjoy. Start now and design a healthy lifestyle that is enjoyable to you and that fits nicely within your dreams.

Below are some reasons why you should live healthfully:

- You will have more energy
- You will feel better and more powerful
- Your mind will be clearer and work more efficiently
- You will have more self confidence
- You will be happier
- You will be capable of doing more
- When you get older, you won't have a bin full of medications that you are required to take every day
- For your family and for the enjoyment of life

Below are some easy tips to living a healthy lifestyle:

- Be physically active in some way
- Get enough rest
- Take supplements

- Stay hydrated by drinking plenty of water
- Involve your family in a healthier lifestyle
- Eat at least two raw servings of veggies or fruit every day (yum!)
- Have your children help you create healthy weekly menus (saves time and money)
- Take time for yourself
- Schedule a lazy day
- Ask for help when you need it
- Schedule alone time
- Go on a date with your husband or loved one
- Keep in touch with family and friends
- Have a support group or a workout buddy
- Have someone who truly cares, that you can cry, rant, vent or just talk to

It's funny that 'exercise' seems like such a negative word, so I won't use it. I do want to share some quick and easy ways to sneak staying fit into your day:

- Balance on one foot while putting on your makeup, socks and shoes
- Do squats while waiting for the microwave
- Do pushups off the cupboard while you are waiting for water to boil
- Stretch or do sit ups on the floor while watching your children bath or while you are watching the news or your favorite sitcom
- Tie your shoes standing and stretch your hamstrings (just keep bending over until you feel a stretch)
- Quickly do 30 sit-ups and 12 pushups before you jump in the shower
- Park in the back row of every parking lot
- Do not use drive up windows
- Be physically active in 10 minute blocks
    - Note: 30 minutes adds up quickly; 10 when you wake up, then 10 midday, and 10 before or after dinner

- Walk everywhere you can instead of using your car
- Plan a walk or a fun activity with your children and/or husband
- Be creative and find things that work for you

Set some healthy goals and add completion dates to them, plan your meals and schedule daily physical activity.

If you aren't taking time to take care of You, for yourself, then do it for the ones you love

Chapter Twenty-Seven

Marriage and Relationships

*"People who care about each other enjoy doing things
for one another. They don't consider it servitude."*
Ann Landers

It is important to have a good relationship with the person you love because it will foster success in all areas of your life.

I believe our spouse or partner is one of the easiest persons to take for granted, to get frustrated with, and to forget that they are your best friend that will stand by you, through thick and thin.

I have some thoughts on ways to have a wonderful and nurturing relationship that I want to share with you:

- Spend quality time together
- Be committed to being happy together
- Learn something new together (try a new sport, visit a museum, etc.)
- Schedule date nights often, either just the two of you or with other adults who you enjoy
- Think and say only positive things about your relationship
- Express appreciation and gratitude by saying "thank you" often
- Acknowledge every good deed
- Do special things for each other regularly
- Surprise each other with small thoughtful gifts or notes
- Compliment each other frequently
- Participate in regular physical touch
- Listen to each other's needs and be supportive
- Find ways to understand each other

- Look at each other's issues from the both sides
- Communicate clearly, without emotion ("My experience was…..")

Be thankful that you have a partner for life; keep your relationship alive and thriving and always nurture it.

❧ *Choose to be happy together* ❧

Chapter Twenty-Eight

Friends

"Close friends contribute to our personal growth. They also contribute to our personal pleasure, making the music sound sweeter, the wine taste richer,
the laughter ring louder because they are there."
Judith Viorst

A good friend will support you in your dreams and will be there when you need them. They will encourage you and give you confidence; they believe in you. They will share in your failures and celebrate your successes.

Some friends may come and go, but each one has taken part in your life and you have shared life changing experiences with each one. With each person that passes through your life, you hold a piece of them, whether you want to or not, the good and the bad.

Below are some of the best things about a good friend:

- They believe in you
- They help you grow
- They will lift your spirits
- They will give you the confidence you need, when you need it
- They will help you get through tough times
- You can be yourself around them
- You can confide in and trust them
- You can count on them to be there when you need to talk, vent, or cry
- They are fun to be with

- They are always honest and trustworthy
- They are supportive
- They never hold grudges against anyone in your life

Friends enrich each other's lives, so value and nurture your relationship, building a close bond. Don't let another day go by without telling a close friend how much they mean to you.

> *I sincerely cannot say enough positive things about having one or more close friends. I have been extremely fortunate to have exceptional friends in my life. They have helped to mold and shape my life and make me the person I am today.*

✎ *Spend time with good friends often, have a lot of fun and clear your mind* ✎

Chapter Twenty-Nine

Building Your Circle of Influence

"Never lose sight of the fact that the most important yardstick of your success
will be how you treat other people - your family, friends, and coworkers,
and even strangers you meet along the way."
Barbara Bush

Every person who you encounter is important. You never know who you will meet that may change your life and eventually may become one of your closest friends.

You will grow personally as you build your circle of influence. Never let an opportunity pass to introduce yourself to someone.

How to build your circle of influence

- Be person of excellence
- Listen
- Help others
- Give good advice
- Give positive feedback
- Make others feel good about themselves
- Show kindness to others
- Be charitable
- Volunteer your time
- Share your knowledge
- Teach and mentor
- Attend seminars and events
- Join groups and forums
- Be open to new ideas

Everything you accomplish requires a relationship of some sort. It may be with family, friends, co-workers, staff, boss, partners, acquaintances, vendors, clients, students, fans, or even a whole audience. Take every opportunity to build new relationships, both personal and in business, because every person is worthy of your attention.

The circle of influence you create will say a lot about you and your credibility

Chapter Thirty

Just for Fun

"When you find yourself stressed, ask yourself one question:
"Will this matter five years from now?"
If yes, then do something about the situation. If no, then let it go."
Catherine Pulsifer

The following lists will lighten your load and make you smile! That is why I am sharing them with you.

Seven things to carry with you to relieve stress:

1. Carry a penny so you can't say "I'm broke."
2. Carry an eraser so you can make all of your mistakes disappear.
3. Carry a rubber band so you can stretch yourself beyond your limits.
4. Carry a string so you can tie things together when they seem to be coming apart.
5. Carry a marble to use if someone says "You have lost your marbles."
6. Carry a star that you can wish upon when it seems your dreams are lost.
7. Carry a 'Hug Me' button so you can get a hug to lift your spirits.

Things you can't recover:

The stone.........after the throw.
The word........after it's said.
The occasion........after it's missed.
The time.........after it's gone.

' '

Ten simple things you can do to brighten your day:

1. Laugh out loud
2. Sing out loud
3. Spend time alone or with a close friend
4. Think of something you are grateful for
5. Give someone a compliment
6. Volunteer
7. Take a nap
8. Go for a walk
9. Eat your favorite dessert
10. Read your favorite magazine
Bonus: Put on some music and dance!

Now you add some things that make you happy.

11. _____

12. _____

13. _____

14. _____

15. _____

Chapter Thirty-One

Self Assessment

*"Because you're human, it is your nature to journey, to discover
that what you've been looking for is all around you.
Very often the grassy spot you seek is right under your feet.
You just need to awaken to that knowledge that's hidden from your
conscious mind. Yes, you're wearing ruby slippers and can go home
anytime you like. For now, embrace this grand adventure."
-Colette Baron-Reid*

Sometimes even after you have clarified your dreams and set your goals, it may feel like something is still missing. That is the purpose for this self assessment. It is fun and it may open some doors to new thinking.

Below are some thought provoking questions to ask yourself:

Health

What are your eating habits?
What are you doing to stay healthy?
Are you getting enough sleep?
What is your optimum weight?
Are you engaged in your favorite recreational activity?

Relationships

Do you have a close family bond?
Do you have a best friend?
Do you have someone you can lean on in times of need?
Do you have someone to share your successes with?

Life

How could you have more fun in life?
What would make your life more pleasurable?
Are you making strides toward your goals?

Financial

What is your debt level?
What is your financial plan for the next year?
What is your financial plan for retirement?

Career

Are you happy with your career or do you want more?
What would you rather be doing?
Are you open to new opportunities?

Personal Growth

What are you doing to promote your personal growth?
If you could learn anything, what would it be?
What would you like to know more about?

Life's purpose

What is your life's purpose?
Have you written your life's purpose?
Does your life's purpose bring you fulfillment?

Final questions

If you continue on your current path, where will you be 5 years
from now?
Where do you want to be headed? Are you on course to get there?
Who can help you reach your dreams and goals?

Now that you have answered some of these questions, you may have opened some new doors for new goals. Having new goals is healthy so go ahead, write another one now!

❧ Enjoy your journey! ❧

Never Give Up

Never give up!

❧ *Thank you for taking your time to read this guide; I feel as though I have accomplished something because I know that when you follow the principles in this guide, your life, and the lives of those around you, will forever be changed positively.* ❧

About the Author

- Shanna Beaman
- Born in Utah
- I love to be with my family
- I enjoy being casual

Family

- Family is more important to me than anything else
- One fabulous husband
- Two wonderful children

My Passions

- Being with my family
- Helping others succeed
- I love to share my experiences and knowledge with others
- I feel a sense of accomplishment when I help others reach their dreams
- I enjoy hearing about the successes others have had in their lives; it inspires me

Working My Way Up

- I have worked full time since I was a teenager. Here is where I came from:
  - As a teenager, I worked at two at different food places, then on an assembly line boxing cookies. I then I held a job assembling medical devices and next, I worked at a women's spa/gym and helped women with their exercise programs and goals.

- In my twenties, I earned my realtor's license and sold real estate for a few years and while selling real estate, I earned my appraiser's license.
- For the next 23 years, I held multiple positions managing offices, earning the title of COO in my last position, managing a company with revenues of $10 million annually.
- I have trained, mentored, and motivated employees, students, current and past members of the *Achieve Your Dreams* program and many other individuals throughout my career.
- I now work from home, mentoring, creating, writing and still working with other companies. This is a huge reward for my hard work and dedication throughout my career, as well as a blessing for my family and me.

If you have any questions, suggestions, or comments, please feel free to contact me at shanna@dustingoffdreams.com

Words of Wisdom

Inspirational Quotes from Women

If you want to accomplish the goals of your life,
you have to begin with the spirit.
Oprah Winfrey

<u>Happiness</u>

"If you can't make it better, you can laugh at it."
Erma Bombeck

' '

"Achievement of your happiness is the only moral purpose of your life,
and that happiness, not pain or mindless self-indulgence, is the proof
of your moral integrity, since it is the proof and the result of your loyalty
to the achievement of your values."
Ayn Rand

' '

"Every time you smile at someone, it is an action of love,
a gift to that person, a beautiful thing."
Mother Teresa

' '

"I hope everyone that is reading this is having a really good day.
And if you are not, just know that in every new minute that
passes you have an opportunity to change that."
Gillian Anderson

' '

"We all have to start with ourselves. It is time to walk the talk.
Take the journey of making very difficult decisions.
Start removing things from your life that are not filling your cup
and adding things that bring joy in to your life."
Lisa Hammond

Dreams

"People need dreams, there's as much nourishment in 'em as food.
Dorothy Gilman

. . . .

"Dreams pass into the reality of action. From the actions stems the dream
again; and this interdependence produces the highest form of living."
Anais Nin

. . . .

"No matter how many goals you have achieved, you must
set your sights on a higher one."
Jessica Savitch

Belief

"Believe in yourself and there will come a day when others will
have no choice but to believe with you."
Cynthia Kersey

. . . .

"No one can make you feel inferior without your consent."
Eleanor Roosevelt

. . . .

"The minute you settle for less than you deserve,
you get even less than you settled for."
Maureen Dowd

ı ı

"Striving for excellence motivates you; striving for perfection is
demoralizing."   Harriet Braiker

Success

"Life is a process of becoming, a combination of states we have to go
through. Where people fail is that they wish to elect a state and remain in
it. This is a kind of death."
Anais Nin

ı ı

"What is success? I think it is a mixture of having a flair for the thing that
you are doing; knowing that it is not enough, that you have got to have
hard work and a certain sense of purpose."
Margaret Thatcher

ı ı

"The ladder of success is best climbed by stepping on the rungs of
opportunity."
Ayn Rand

ı ı

"Success doesn't come to you, you go to it."
Marva Collins

ı ı

"Getting ahead in a difficult profession requires avid faith in yourself.
You must be able to sustain yourself against staggering blows.
There is no code of conduct to help beginners.
That is why some people with mediocre talent, but with great inner drive,
go much further than people with vastly superior talent."
Sophia Loren

ı ı

"You may have a fresh start any moment you choose, for this thing that
we call 'failure' is not the falling down, but the staying down."
Mary Pickford

ı ı

"If you want success, then don't rely on other people to do what YOU can
do!" Sasha Azevedo

Spiritual/Well being

"Find something that you're really interested in doing in your life. Pursue
it, set goals, and commit yourself to excellence. Do the best you can."
Chris Evert

ı ı

"Let's choose today to quench our thirst for the 'good life' we think others
lead by acknowledging the good that already exists in our lives. We can
then offer the universe the gift of our grateful hearts."
Sarah Ban Breathnach

ı ı

"It is for us to pray not for tasks equal to our powers, but for powers equal
to our tasks, to go forward with a great desire forever beating at the door
of our hearts as we travel toward our distant goal."

Helen Keller

"A field of flowers is planted one flower at a time."
Shanna Beaman

Obstacles

"Greatness is not measured by what a man or woman accomplishes, but by the opposition he or she has overcome to reach his goals."
Dorothy Height

ı ı

"Obstacles are those frightful things you see when you take your eyes off the goal."
Hannah More

ı ı

"Life's up and downs provide windows of opportunity to determine your values and goals. Think of using all obstacles as stepping stones to build the life you want."
Marsha Sinetar

Relationships/Family

"Children make your life important."
Erma Bombeck

ı ı

"I believe people are in our lives for a reason.
We're here to learn from each other."
Gillian Anderson

ı ı

"Be of service. Whether you make yourself available to a friend or co-worker, or you make time every month to do volunteer work, there is nothing that harvests more of a feeling of empowerment than being of service to someone in need." - Gillian Anderson

' '

"Cherish your human connections - your relationships with friends and family."
Barbara Bush

' '

"I believe that you should gravitate to people who are doing productive and positive things with their lives."
Nadia Comaneci

Persistence

"Being defeated is often a temporary condition.
Giving up is what makes it permanent."
Marilyn vos Savant

' '

"We gain strength, and courage, and confidence by each experience in which we really stop to look fear in the face...we must do that which we think we cannot."
Eleanor Roosevelt

' '

"Learning is not attained by chance.
It must be sought for with ardor and attended to with diligence."
Abigail Adams

Motivation

"You're alive. Do something.
The directive in life, the moral imperative was so uncomplicated.
It could be expressed in single words, not complete sentences.
It sounded like this: Look. Listen. Choose. Act."
Barbara Hall

"People think that at the top there isn't much room. They tend to think of
it as an Everest. My message is that there is tons of room at the top."
Margaret Thatcher

"Life is to be lived. If you have to support yourself, you had bloody well
better find some way that is going to be interesting. And you don't do that
by sitting around wondering about yourself."
Katharine Hepburn

"Disciplining yourself to do what you know is right and importance,
although difficult, is the highroad to pride, self-esteem, and personal
satisfaction."
Margaret Thatcher

"We've observed that people who stall in their personal growth work
often have counterproductive soft addictions that stand in their way of
growth and having the life they say they want. It can be a simple thing,
such as watching TV instead of finishing a project."
Judith Wright

"You end up as you deserve. In old age you must put up with the face,
the friends, the health, and the children you have earned."
Judith Viorst

Information

You will find all of the forms in this book posted on my website and you may print off as many as you need.

Go to www.dustingoffdreams.com and click on the Tools tab.
Click on Living your Dreams and enter the password: dreamweaving

If you have any questions, suggestions, or comments, please feel free to contact me at shanna@dustingoffdreams.com

One last thing, please share your success stories with me; I would love to hear them!

Extra forms can be found on the following pages.   Please feel free to make additional copies of them for your personal use.

Well Rounded

Financial
10 9 8 7 6 5 4 3 2 1

Relationships
1 2 3 4 5 6 7 8 9 10

You

Health
1 2 3 4 5 6 7 8 9 10

Spiritual
1 2 3 4 5 6 7 8 9 10

Self Improvement
1
2
3
4
5
6
7
8
9
10

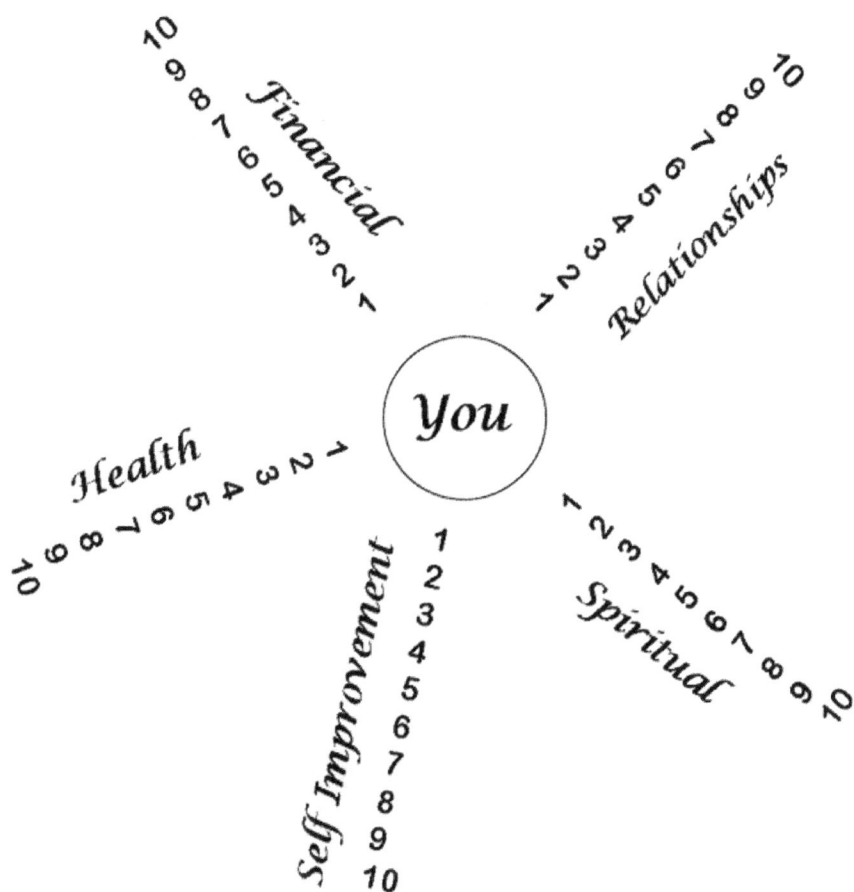

How well rounded is your life?

In each area of life, circle the number that best describes where you feel you are. One being the farthest from your best and ten stating there is no room for improvement. Now connect the numbers and make a circle.

How bumpy is your circle?

Well Rounded

Financial
10 9 8 7 6 5 4 3 2 1

Relationships
1 2 3 4 5 6 7 8 9 10

You

Health
1 2 3 4 5 6 7 8 9 10

Spiritual
1 2 3 4 5 6 7 8 9 10

Self Improvement
1
2
3
4
5
6
7
8
9
10

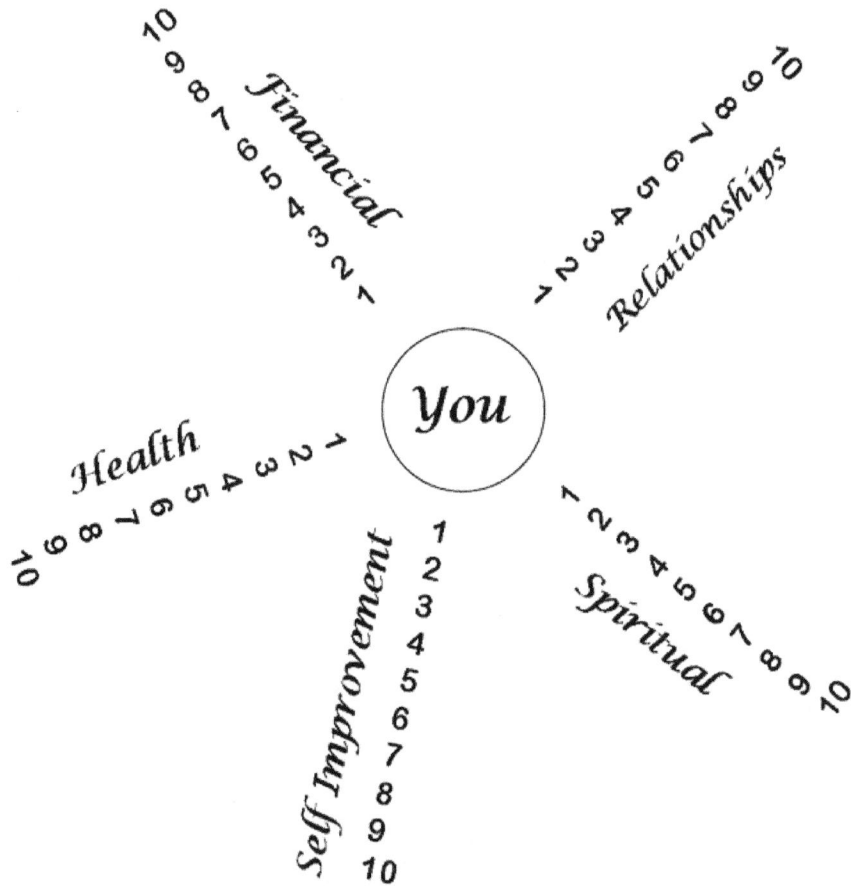

How well rounded is your life?

In each area of life, circle the number that best describes where you feel you are. One being the farthest from your best and ten stating there is no room for improvement. Now connect the numbers and make a circle.

How bumpy is your circle?

List five dreams.

_____

_____

_____

_____

_____

What is your purpose for each dream?

_____

_____

_____

_____

_____

My Dream: (positive and present tense)

_____
_____
_____

Deadline ☐   Realistic ☐   Exclusive ☐   Attainable ☐   Measurable ☐ Specific ☐

Deadline Date:
_____

Benefits from Achieving this Goal:

_____
_____
_____

Possible Obstacles:

_____
_____
_____

Possible Solutions:

_____
_____
_____

Major Action Items:

_____
_____
_____
_____

Reward(s)
_____

My Dream: (positive and present tense)

_____

_____

_____

Deadline □   Realistic □   Exclusive □   Attainable □   Measurable □ Specific □

Deadline Date:

_____

Benefits from Achieving this Goal:

_____

_____

_____

Possible Obstacles:

_____

_____

_____

Possible Solutions:

_____

_____

_____

Major Action Items:

_____

_____

_____

_____

Reward(s)

My Dream: (positive and present tense)

_____

_____

_____

Deadline ☐　Realistic ☐　Exclusive ☐　Attainable ☐　Measurable ☐　Specific ☐

Deadline Date:
_____

Benefits from Achieving this Goal:

_____

_____

_____

Possible Obstacles:

_____

_____

_____

Possible Solutions:

_____

_____

_____

Major Action Items:

_____

_____

_____

_____

Reward(s)
_____

Dream Steps

Priority	To-Do	Completion Date

Dream Steps

Priority	To-Do		Completion Date

Commitment
To Myself

I commit to pursue my dreams by taking control of my life and making time for dream achievement.

I commit to clarify my goals and write them down.

I commit to Dream Weave every day.

I commit to take at least one action step each day, no matter how small.

I believe in myself and my dreams.

My dreams will become reality.

_____

Signature

_____

Date

Commitment
To Myself

_____

_____

_____

_____

_____

_____

_____

_____

Signature

_____

Date

Creating Good Habits

Write your new habit: _____

_____

What are the benefits of this new habit?_____

_____

What are the obstacles to creating this new habit?_____

_____

What are your solutions to overcome the obstacles?_____

_____

What are the action steps you must take?_____

_____

Deadline_____

Eliminating Bad Habits

Write your bad habit: _____

_____

What are the benefits of eliminating this habit?_____

_____

What are the obstacles to overcoming this habit?_____

_____

What are your solutions to overcome the obstacles?_____

_____

What are the action steps you must take?_____

_____

Deadline_____

Creating Empowering Beliefs

Write your limiting belief: _____

_____

Why do you believe this?_____

_____

What actions will you take to overcome this?_____

_____

How will you feel when you eliminate this limiting belief?_____

_____

Write your new empowering belief:_____

_____

Creating Empowering Beliefs

Write your limiting belief: _____

_____

Why do you believe this?_____

_____

What actions will you take to overcome this?_____

_____

How will you feel when you eliminate this limiting belief?_____

_____

Write your new empowering belief:_____

_____

What's Great About Me?

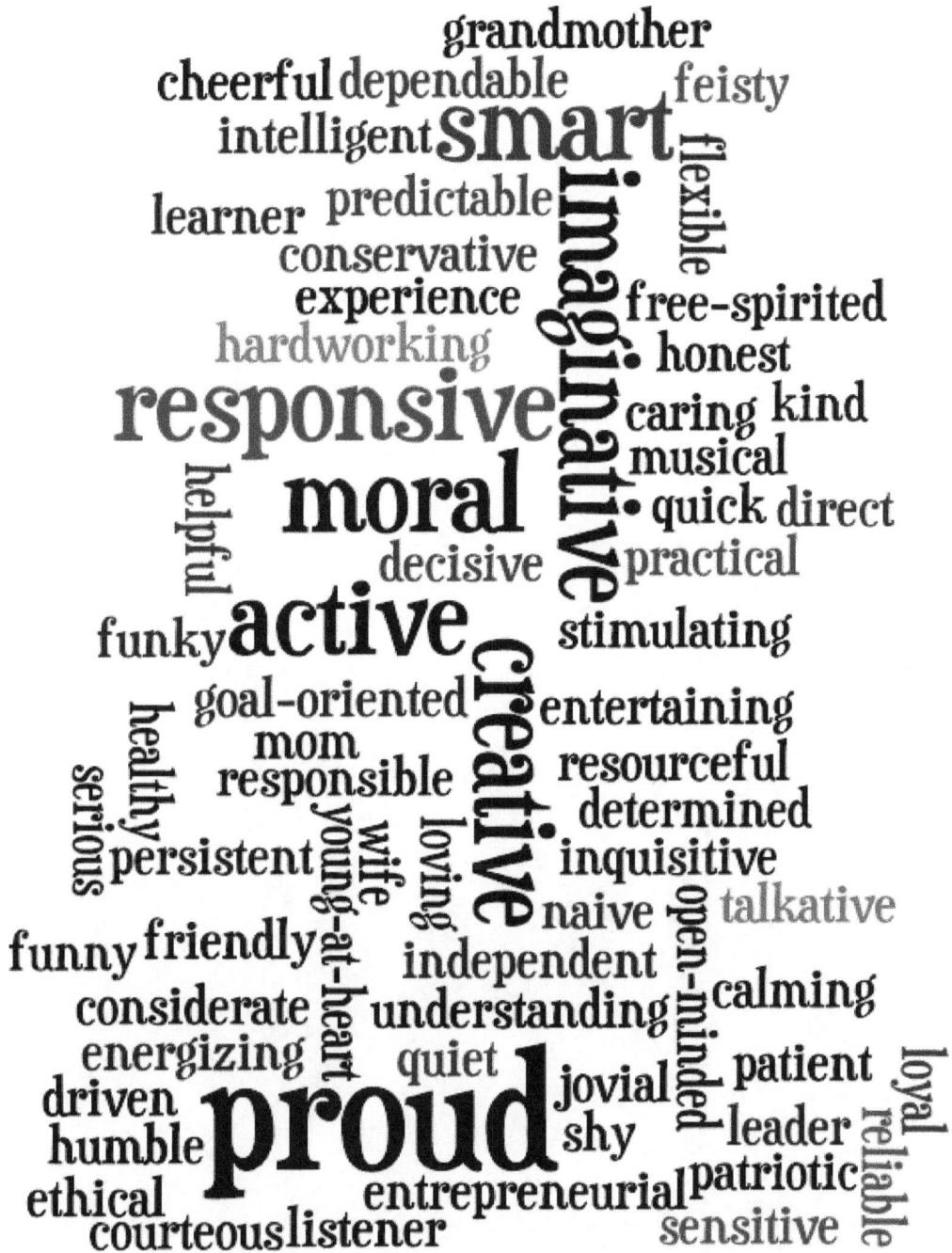

grandmother
cheerful dependable feisty
intelligent **smart** flexible
learner predictable imaginative
conservative
experience free-spirited
hardworking honest
responsive caring kind
musical
helpful **moral** quick direct
decisive practical
funky **active** stimulating
goal-oriented creative entertaining
healthy mom resourceful
serious responsible determined
persistent inquisitive
wife loving naive talkative
funny friendly independent open-minded calming
considerate understanding
energizing quiet jovial patient loyal
driven **proud** shy leader reliable
humble patriotic
ethical entrepreneurial sensitive
courteous listener

Print a bookmark to keep your commitment to yourself in front of you.
Fill in the spaces to remind you of the commitments you have promised
yourself.

*Commitment
to myself*

*Commitment
to myself*

www.ingramcontent.com/pod-product-compliance
Lightning Source LLC
LaVergne TN
LVHW061223060426
835509LV00012B/1408